true meditation

ADYASHANTI

true meditation

discover the freedom of pure awareness

SOUNDS TRUE
awakening wisdom

Sounds True, Inc., Boulder CO 80306

Published 2006
Printed in Canada

11

ISBN-10: 1-59179-467-6
ISBN-13: 978-1-59179-467-7

Library of Congress Control Number: 2006928851

Table of Contents

PART TWO

Editor's Introduction

Each of our lives is a kind of spiritual laboratory in which we test the teachings we encounter in the fire of our own experience. Ultimately, what matters are not the truths other people tell us or the practices that we are able to mimic, but the spiritual discoveries we make through personal investigation.

When I first spoke with Adyashanti (whose name literally means "primordial peace"), I knew I was speaking with a spiritual teacher who had made some very real and personal discoveries. Although he claimed to have "woken up out of Zen," it was his longtime Zen teacher, Arvis Justi, who encouraged him to begin teaching in 1996 at the age of thirty-four. Hearing that people often experienced breakthrough insights in his presence, I knew I wanted to add his input into the spiritual laboratory of my life.

So, in November 2004, I attended a five-day retreat with Adyashanti. During this retreat, Adyashanti gave talks during which retreatants had the opportunity to converse with him publicly about their innermost questions and concerns. We also spent four to five hours each day in silent sitting. During this time, we were to engage in what Adya calls True Meditation. At the retreat, the basic instruction we received to orient ourselves during these silent sittings was two words: No manipulation.

As someone who has spent more than twenty years attending various kinds of meditation retreats and experimenting with dozens of different techniques and approaches, I felt a bit baffled. "No manipulation? That's it?" Could I slouch? What about my discursive mind? Was this really a form of meditation, or was Adya simply giving us permission to space out? What is "True Meditation," anyway?

In addition to receiving the instruction "No manipulation," there was a one-page handout we could read and contemplate. "Thank God," I thought. "Everyone else here may be familiar with Adya and this approach, but I need more information." Maybe the handout would help. Here's what it said:

True Meditation

True Meditation has no direction, goals, or method. All methods aim at achieving a certain state of mind. All states are limited, impermanent, and conditioned. Fascination with states leads only to bondage and dependency. True Meditation is abidance as primordial consciousness.

True Meditation appears in consciousness spontaneously when awareness is not fixated on objects of perception. When you first start to meditate, you notice that awareness is always focused on some object: on thoughts, bodily sensations, emotions, memories, sounds, etc. This is because the mind is conditioned to focus and contract upon objects. Then the mind compulsively interprets what it is aware of (the object) in a mechanical and distorted way. It begins to draw conclusions and make assumptions according to past conditioning.

In True Meditation all objects are left to their natural functioning. This means that no effort should be made to manipulate or suppress any object of awareness. In true meditation the emphasis is on being awareness: not on being aware of objects, but on resting as primordial awareness itself. Primordial awareness (consciousness) is the source in which all objects arise and subside. As you gently relax into awareness, into listening, the mind's compulsive contraction around objects will fade. Silence of being will come more clearly into consciousness as a welcoming to rest and abide. An attitude of open receptivity, free of any goal or anticipation, will facilitate the presence of silence and stillness to be revealed as your natural condition.

Silence and stillness are not states and therefore cannot be produced or created. Silence is the non-state in which all states arise and subside. Silence, stillness, and awareness are not states and can never be perceived in their totality as objects. Silence is itself the eternal witness without form or attributes. As you rest more profoundly as the witness, all objects take on their natural functionality, and awareness becomes free of the mind's compulsive contractions and identifications, and returns to its natural non-state of Presence.

The simple yet profound question, "Who Am I?," can then reveal one's self not to be the endless tyranny of the ego-personality, but objectless Freedom of Being—Primordial Consciousness in which all states and all objects come and go as manifestations of the Eternal Unborn Self that YOU ARE.

Folding up this handout and sticking it in the pocket of my jeans, I spent the five-day retreat alternately practicing the meditation techniques I was familiar with and simply relaxing, listening, and being without manipulation. But at the end of the retreat, I had to admit I had far more questions than answers. What is the role of technique in meditation? Does this approach work for meditators of all levels, or only for advanced practitioners who have already spent years familiarizing themselves with quieting the mind? What about posture and the physical and emotional pain that can often arise during periods of meditation?

Filled with questions, I asked Adyashanti if he would be willing to work with Sounds True to create a teaching program on True Meditation. He agreed, and this book and CD combination is the result. I handed Adya a list of questions and he responded by giving two dharma talks on the topic of True Meditation: one talk on "Allowing Everything To Be As It Is" and a second talk on "Meditative Self-Inquiry." He also recorded two guided meditations (on the enclosed CD) so that listeners can explore these teachings in their own introspective way.

According to Adyashanti, spiritual discoveries are self-authenticating. What matters most is not what others affirm but what you realize in your own being. It is my hope that this book and CD offering on True Meditation will further your own process of genuine discovery, for the benefit of all beings.

Tami Simon
Publisher, Sounds True
May 2006, Boulder, Colorado

PART ONE

Allow Everything To Be As It Is

We're going to investigate the whole notion of meditation, what meditation is, why we meditate, and what meditation can lead to. I want to explore what I call True Meditation, which you'll come to realize as I describe it is actually something quite specific and also something quite different from the kind of meditation that most people are used to hearing about. But first, a little personal history.

Ending the War with the Mind

I came from the Zen Buddhist tradition, and in the Zen tradition, there is a long history in which the primary practice is meditation. In Zen, you often meditate for hours a day in the seated meditation posture for a prescribed period of time. And what I found out through many years of practice in this style of meditation is that I actually wasn't particularly good at it. I think a lot of people find when they first begin to meditate that they're not particularly good at it—their minds are busy, their bodies want to be twitching, and it's hard for them to calm down and be quiet. So my experience from the beginning was that meditation was actually very difficult for me to do. And I find for a lot of people it is something that is actually very difficult for them to do.

So I found myself sitting, on various retreats and at home. At home I would sit for maybe half an hour or an hour a day, sometimes longer. I would go on retreats and sit for much, much longer periods of time. And very often my meditation was actually anything but meditation. It was a lot of struggle, a lot of trying to calm my mind, a lot of trying to control my thoughts, and a lot of trying to be still, without much success—except for a few magical moments when meditation just seemed to happen. Because I wasn't particularly gifted at meditation initially—at being able to control my mind and enter into a meditative state—after some years I realized that I needed to find a different way to meditate. The approach I was using clearly wasn't working. This is when I began my investigation into what I call True Meditation.

One day I was speaking with my teacher, and she said, "If you try to win the war with your mind, you'll be at war forever." That really struck me. At that moment I realized I had been viewing meditation as a battle with my mind. I was trying to control my mind, to pacify my mind, to try to get my mind to be quiet. Suddenly I thought, "My goodness, forever is an awfully long time. I must come up with a whole different way of looking at this." If continuing this way meant I was going to be at war with my mind indefinitely, I needed to find a way not to be at war with my mind. Without even knowing it I started to investigate, in a quiet and very deep way, what it would be like not to be at war with my own mind, with what I felt, with my whole human experience.

I started to meditate in a different way. I let go of the idea of what meditation was supposed to be. My mind had had a lot of ideas about meditation. It was supposed to be peaceful; I was supposed to feel a particular way, mostly calm. Meditation was supposed to lead me into some deep state of being. But because I could not master the technique of meditation as it was being taught to me, I had to discover a different way of meditating, one that wasn't oriented around a technique. So I would sit down and let my experience simply be, in a very deep way. I started to let go of trying to control my experience. That became the beginning of discovering for myself what True Meditation is. From that point on, that shift—moving from trying to perfect a technique or discipline to actually letting go of technique and discipline—started to inform the way I engage in meditation.

An Attitude of Innocence

Our ideas about meditation are usually colored by our past conditioning—what we've learned about it, what we think meditation is, where we think it should lead. Meditation can serve a whole array of agendas. Some people meditate for better physical or emotional health or to still their bodies or minds. Some people meditate to open up certain subtle energy channels within their bodies, often called *chakras*. Some people meditate to develop love, to develop compassion. Some people meditate in order to achieve altered states of consciousness. Other people meditate to try and gain certain spiritual or psychic powers—what they call *siddhis*. And then there's meditation as an aid to spiritual awakening and enlightenment. It's this kind of meditation—meditation that is an aid to spiritual awakening and enlightenment—that really interests me. It's what True Meditation is all about.

It doesn't matter whether one is brand new to meditation or has been meditating for a long time. What I have found is that history doesn't really make any difference. What matters is the attitude with which we engage the process of meditation. The most important thing is that we come to meditation with an open attitude, an attitude that is truly innocent, by which I mean an attitude that's not colored by the past, by what we've heard about meditation through culture, through the media, or through our various spiritual and religious traditions. We need to approach the notion of meditation in a way that is fresh and innocent.

As a spiritual teacher, I've met a lot of people who have meditated for many, many years. One of the most common things I hear from many of these people is that, despite having meditated for all this time, they feel essentially untransformed. The deep inner transformation—the spiritual revelation—that meditation offers is something that eludes a lot of people, even those who are longtime practitioners. There are actually good and specific reasons why some meditation practices, including the kind of meditation that I was once engaged in, do not lead to this promised state of transformation. The main reason is actually extraordinarily simple and therefore easy to miss: we approach meditation with the wrong attitude. We carry out our meditation with an attitude of control and manipulation, and that is the very reason our meditation leads us to what feels like a dead end. The awakened state of being, the enlightened state of being, can also be called the *natural* state of being. How can control and manipulation possibly lead us to our natural state?

Relinquishing Control and Manipulation

Enlightenment is, in the end, nothing more than the natural state of being. If you strip it of all the complex terminology and all the complex jargon, enlightenment is simply returning to our natural state of being. A natural state, of course, means a state which is not contrived, a state that requires no effort or discipline to maintain, a state of being which is not enhanced by any sort of manipulation of mind or body—in other words, a state that is completely natural, completely spontaneous. Herein lies one of the reasons why meditation often leads to a dead end. Many meditation techniques, when you look at them closely, are a means of control. As long as the mind is controlling and guiding our experience, it is unlikely to lead us to a natural state. A natural state is one in which we are not controlled by the mind. When the mind is involved in control and manipulation, it can lead to various states of consciousness: you might learn how to still your mind, or you might come into psychic powers. You can achieve a lot of things through a style of meditation that is basically technique-oriented or manipulation-oriented. But what you can't do is come upon your own natural and spontaneous way of being.

This seems like the most obvious thing in the world. Anyone can tell you that you're not going to come to a natural and spontaneous way of being through inner control and manipulation, yet somehow this truth eludes us. It eluded me for years. The fault isn't necessarily in the style of meditation or even in the technique, although the technique we use can have a profound influence. *The problem lies in the attitude with which we engage meditation.* If our attitude is an attitude of control and manipulation—if we take the approach that we are going to master a discipline—then the attitude gets in the way. It's actually the mind or the ego that is meditating. And, of course, when we are talking about enlightenment or spiritual awakening we are talking about awakening *from* the mind, awakening *from* the ego. In what I call True Meditation, this tendency of the mind to control and manipulate and be disciplined is abandoned from the very beginning. This letting go of control and manipulation is the foundation of True Meditation. As funny as it sounds, the extraordinarily simple beginning to meditation is to let go of control, let go of manipulation.

When most people sit down to meditate the first thing they think is, "Okay, how do I control my mind?" That's what I am calling manipulation. Manipulation is a strong word, but I am using it to get your attention, to call attention to the fact that when we sit down to meditate and ask ourselves, "Okay, how am I going to control my mind? How am I going to come to peace? How am I going to come to stillness?", what the mind is actually doing is asking, "How do I control myself so that I feel better?" And you can learn to control your mind and quiet your mind and your body by applying a controlling technique. For a while it might feel good. But when we control our minds in order to obtain a certain state of peace or tranquility, it's very much like getting someone to be quiet by taping their mouth shut. You've succeeded in getting that person to be quiet, but you've done it through a very manipulative technique. What good will come of getting that person to be quiet by taping their mouth shut? As soon as you take the tape off they are going to have a few things to say, aren't they? They're going to have an awful lot to say! I think anybody who has meditated knows the experience of entering into meditation and achieving a certain control of mind, a control of body. It may feel very, very good. The experience may even feel profound. But then you stop meditating—you get up off the cushion or the chair, you stand up—and immediately your mind starts to chatter again. We experience a type of meditative quietness through control, but as soon as we let go of control the mind is off and running again. Everything reverts to the way it was before. Most meditators are all too familiar with this dilemma. We may achieve a certain state of peace when we are meditating, but when we stop meditating the peace eludes us once again.

Real meditation is not about mastering a technique; it's about letting go of control. This is meditation. Anything else is actually a form of concentration. Meditation and concentration are two different things. Concentration is a discipline; concentration is a way in which we are actually directing or guiding or controlling our experience. Meditation is letting go of control, letting go of guiding our experience in any way whatsoever. The foundation of True Meditation is that we are letting go of control.

For a human being to let go of control is actually an immense thing. It sounds easy to say, "Just let go of control." But for most human beings, our entire psychological structure, our entire psychological self, our egos, are made up almost entirely of control. To ask a mind or an ego to let go of control, then, is a revolutionary idea. When we let go, even for a moment, certain hidden fears and hesitations arise. "What if I let go of control," the mind says, "and nothing happens? What if I sit down to meditate, letting everything be as it is, and nothing happens?" This is usually why we grab on to some technique or to some discipline, because the mind is afraid that if it lets go of control, nothing will happen.

What I am suggesting in True Meditation is that we actually *see*, that we look at meditation as a way to investigate. True Meditation really isn't a new technique so much as it is a way of investigating for yourself—in your own body, in your own mind, upon your own authority, upon the authority of your own experience—what happens when you start to relinquish control and allow everything to be as it is. What happens when you allow your experience to be exactly as it is without trying to change it. Instead of a technique, True Meditation is actually a means of investigation. What happens when we actually let go of control and manipulation?

Moving Beyond the Meditator

The second aspect of True Meditation is meditative self-inquiry. Meditative self-inquiry is the practice of introducing a question—a spiritual question of power and significance—into the meditative state of mind. We are not just asking any old question; we are asking questions of real worth, questions that have the power to penetrate through layers of conditioning to reach our essential nature. The most powerful question we can ask is simply, "What am I? Who is the meditator?" This question undercuts all the ways the ego tries to control experience. It asks, "Who is controlling experience? Who is meditating?" One of the essential reasons for meditating is to go beyond the meditator—to go beyond the ego or mind. As long as the meditator is in control, there is very little possibility of moving beyond the mind or ego. This is why, in True Meditation, the practice is to let go of the meditator. The very first instant of meditation is an invitation to let go of control and to allow everything to be as it is. This practice disengages the meditator. If the meditator is doing anything, it's simply letting go of control, letting go of trying to change anything.

When I say "meditator," it is important to realize that the meditator is the one who is controlling. The meditator is the one who is trying—the manipulator, the one exerting effort. And in most forms of meditation, the meditator is very much engaged. The mind is getting something to do and something to master—and the mind loves having something to do! It loves having something to master, because then it gets to remain in control. But for a form of meditation to be relevant in terms of spiritual awakening—in terms of awakening to the true nature of who and what we are—we must go beyond the meditator, beyond the controller, beyond the manipulator.

Do Meditative Techniques Have Any Value?

A lot of people, myself included, come from various traditions where meditation is taught as a technique. We are taught various forms of control, such as focusing on the breath or focusing on various parts of the body. In the Zen tradition, we often focus just slightly below the navel. Often we are taught to sit in a certain posture, with our backs straight, and to breathe in a particular way. These techniques and disciplines have been taught for hundreds and thousands of years, and I am not suggesting that they have no value or merit. They do have value and merit. What I am saying, however, is that it's when we start to let go of these techniques, when we start to let go of this focusing, that we can approach our natural state of being. Often these techniques obscure our natural state of consciousness. When I am leading a retreat I often begin by saying that I know different people have different ways of meditating and of centering themselves. Some people follow their breath. Some people say a mantra. Some people do deep breathing. Some people do visualization practices. I say to the group that to engage these techniques at the beginning of a meditation session is fine. These are perfectly appropriate ways of bringing the mind into the present. They allow you to gather the psychic energy and the resources of the active mind and to pool them into right here and right now. And yet what I suggest is that, in any given period of meditation, we also take time to let go of whatever technique we're using. If I'm following my breath, I also experiment with what happens when I let go of following my breath. What happens when I let go of watching my mind? Or saying my mantra? These practices may help us gather our attention into the moment; that is their primary value. But once our attention is in the present, then the invitation is to let go of these techniques and to start to investigate our natural state of being.

And so I have found that often, if we are not careful, these ancient traditions and techniques—many of which I myself was taught, and which have great value—become an end instead of a *means* to an end. People end up with what is simply a discipline. They end up watching their breath for years and years and years, becoming perfect at watching their breath. But in the end spirituality is not about watching the breath. It's about waking up from the dream of separateness to the truth of unity. That's what it's about, and this can get forgotten if we adhere too closely to technique. So we might start with a little technique, a little watching the breath, saying a prayer, saying a mantra, using a visualization. But my suggestion is always that we should move relatively soon into a curiosity about what happens when we allow everything to be as it is. At this point we start to transition from control of mind into True Meditation. It's a revolutionary transition. A lot of people I've met have forgotten that transition, forgotten to let that transition happen. They've forgotten that the point comes relatively soon when you can—and should—let go of control.

True Meditation Begins with Resting in the Natural State

In True Meditation, we start from the foundation of letting everything be as it is. In True Meditation we are not moving toward the natural state, or trying to create the natural state; we actually start at the natural state from the very beginning. This is what I discovered all those years ago when I started to let go of the meditator, the controller, when I sat down and simply allowed everything to be as it was. What I realized very quickly was that the peace and stillness I was trying to attain were already there. All I had to do was stop trying to attain them. All I had to do was to sit down and allow my experience to be as it was.

Like most people, when I sat I sometimes felt good and peaceful. Other times I would be agitated, upset, or anxious. Sometimes I would be sad, and sometimes I would be happy. I felt all the various human emotions while I was sitting. What I realized was that when I allowed my experience to be as it was, and made no effort to change it, an underlying natural state of being started to rise into consciousness. An uncontaminated, unmanufactured state of consciousness would start to arise, very simply and very naturally. I would call it a very *innocent* state of consciousness, because it wasn't derived from effort or discipline. I discovered that the natural state, our natural state of being, is not an altered state of consciousness. So many people associate meditation with altered states of consciousness. Yet this is a profound misunderstanding about the potential of meditation. The potential I'm talking about is spiritual awakening, awakening to the realization of what you and everything actually is, the oneness of all. We are taught, or we assume, that to perceive everything as one and to perceive yourself as not separate is to enter an altered state of consciousness. And yet, as it turns out, the truth is just the opposite. To perceive everything as one is not an altered state of consciousness. It's an *unaltered* state of consciousness; it's the natural state of consciousness. By comparison, everything else is an altered state.

When we think of meditation we need to let go of the idea that enlightenment is an altered state of consciousness that we can somehow attain. Practiced meditators know that if you meditate hard enough and long enough, you will occasionally enter into altered states of consciousness. There are all sorts of them. Happiness is an altered state of consciousness. Sadness is an altered state of consciousness. Depression is an altered state of consciousness. Then, of course, there are all the mystical states of consciousness: merging with the cosmos is an altered state of consciousness; feeling your consciousness expand is an altered state of consciousness. There are many varieties of altered states of consciousness. Most people think enlightenment is some altered state of consciousness. This is a profound misunderstanding. Enlightenment is the natural state of consciousness, the innocent state of consciousness, that state which is uncontaminated by the movement of thought, uncontaminated by control or manipulation of mind. This is really what enlightenment is all about. We cannot come upon this truth of our nature through manipulation. We cannot move beyond what I call the false identity, the egoic identity, by trying to change. We can only start to allow consciousness to wake up from its identification with thought and feeling, with body and mind and personality, by allowing ourselves to rest in the natural state from the very beginning.

The Ultimate Act of Faith

Spiritual awakening does not come about through any sort of intellectual understanding. We cannot arrive at our true nature through words, through concepts, through ideas, or through theology. None of those means reveal our true nature. It's extraordinarily important to realize that when the mind is trying to understand, when the mind is trying to grasp an intellectual comprehension of ultimate reality, the mind is simply trying to remain in control. It's an intellectual form of mind control, and it needs to be let go of as well. Which isn't to say that the mind plays no part in spiritual awakening; this is also a common misunderstanding of spirituality. The mind plays a vital role. Thought itself plays an important role. Later I will talk about how we use the mind in the form of spiritual inquiry. In spiritual inquiry we are actually engaging the mind, in order to go beyond the mind.

So I am not suggesting that mind and thought are ultimately a problem. It's our *attachment* to mind that is a problem. It is an illusory pursuit to look to concepts and ideas in order to find truth, to find peace, to find that which will liberate us. When we let go of the thinking mind, we become open to insight—to what in spirituality we might call revelation, or the spontaneous arising of a deep wisdom or a deep knowing. It arises in the mind but does not derive from the mind. It is an "Aha" experience—an instantaneous understanding. When you think, "Aha! I understand that," it's not a matter of logical thought. It's something that just registers in the mind, and in the body, and has the nature of a revelation. And so again, to get access to this level of insight, we start by letting go of control, even control of the mind. We enter into a natural state of being. In a sense, True Meditation is the ultimate act of faith. Because to sit down and let everything be as it already is—to let go of control, to let go of manipulation—is itself a very deep act of faith. It's also a deep act of investigation.

What happens when we actually let go of this control? What happens when we allow everything to be exactly as it is? This question is the foundation of all spirituality. Until we can allow everything to be as it is, in the deepest possible way, in the most profound way, we are still involved in control. In true spirituality and in True Meditation we are letting go of this control from the beginning. We are not pumping energy into the ego, into the mind, into the controller, into the manipulator. We are actually letting go of effort, which is a revolutionary idea to most people—that we can meditate in such a way that we are not making an effort. This does not mean we are being lazy or going to sleep. But letting go of control, letting everything be as it is, is a means of letting go of effort. So when I say that we let go of control, that we let everything be as it is, it is the same as saying we let go of making an effort. We find out what happens in our consciousness when we let go of effort, when we let go of discipline. And we can start to see in our own experience that there's a certain vitality that comes into consciousness. It's almost like a light gets turned on within, simply because we let go of effort and control. Something that is innocent and beautiful and uncontaminated starts to arise in consciousness; it starts to arise all on its own and all by itself. And this is quite different from what most of us have been taught. We've been taught that to enter a natural state of consciousness we must learn to control and discipline ourselves; what I am saying is that it's just the opposite. You come into the natural state by letting go of control by letting go of effort and resting in a state of vividness. It's very simple. It couldn't be simpler. Sit down; let everything be as it already is. You can even ask yourself a very simple question, right from the very beginning: "Is it not true that the peace and the stillness I am trying to attain through meditation are already here, right now?" Then look for yourself. When we look for ourselves, we come to see that yes, indeed, peace and stillness are totally natural states, and they are already happening. At that point all you have to do is notice it and then give yourself to it. Find out what happens when you give yourself to the peace that already is, to the stillness that already is. This is the investigation.

Posture and Gaze

One of the most common questions I get when I introduce this teaching on True Meditation is whether it matters how you sit. Do you need to sit in meditation with a straight, erect spine, or can you relax in an easy chair or sit on a couch? My response is that it is preferable not to lie down—because people have a tendency to go to sleep when they lie down—but that, otherwise, sitting in a certain posture is not the most important thing to me. I understand that a lot of traditions emphasize proper posture. The Zen tradition I came from emphasizes posture quite a bit. And there are good reasons for emphasizing posture. Certain postures actually open us emotionally and physically. When our posture is open, when our spine is erect and our hands are not crossed in front of us, we feel more open. There is a natural sense of openness in such a posture. There are various physical positions that spiritual traditions use to foster an inner sense of openness and an attitude of openness. But what I have found over the years is that while proper posture is useful, what often happens is that the spiritual seeker's mind gets so focused on perfecting and maintaining a particular posture that the result doesn't lead to openness. Instead, it often leads to a hypersensitivity about the perfection of one's posture.

Again, it comes back to our attitude. What's important is that we approach meditation with an underlying attitude of ease and openness and relaxation. We need to move beyond the idea that awakening or enlightenment can only happen if our posture is correct, because that's simply not true. Awakening and enlightenment can happen to straight, erect meditators and slumpy, slouchy meditators who sit out on a lawn chair or however they are drawn to sit. Again, it is the attitude with which we meditate that is important. Are we open? Do we sit with ease? Is our approach very simple? In other words, does our posture allow us to forget the body? Not to dissociate from it, but just to leave it alone?

Another thing that people often ask me is whether they should have their eyes open or closed. Again, various traditions will emphasize different things. Some traditions say you should meditate with your eyes open. Others encourage you to keep them closed. As a teacher, I am more interested in what you are drawn to. What are you drawn to when you take away what you *think* you should do, or what you think you shouldn't do? When you take away the authority that you've learned from somewhere else and reconnect with what's really intimately yours, with that which wasn't given to you by something or somebody else? Many of us have so much knowledge of teachings and instructions that after a while we become disconnected from what's intimately ours, from our own natural and spontaneous wisdom. And so I am always trying to reconnect people immediately, from the very beginning, with what's intimately theirs. What's true for you? If you want to meditate with your eyes open, keep your eyes open. If you prefer them closed, close them. Experiment, switch between the two. If you are sleepy, it is a good idea to keep your eyes open. It helps to wake you up a bit. Other times you'll have your eyes open and you'll feel they want to close—not because you are sleepy, but because they just want to close. And if they want to close, then let them close. Feel your way through. Become very intimate with your own experience.

Effortless Effort

Another common question has to do with effort and effortlessness. I talk a lot about ease and effortlessness, and sometimes people get confused and think I am saying you should almost be lazy. Meditating in an effortless way is not the same as being lazy, and it's not the same as being hazy. In fact, one of the most beautiful and profound instructions my teacher used to give me when I talked to her about meditation came in the form of a question: Is it vivid? Is it alive? This is a very good instruction. If we're simply making no effort in a way that's lazy, then our meditation gets dreamy and foggy. It's almost like we're in a trance state or even in a drug-induced state. That's not what is meant by effortlessness. Effortless doesn't mean no effort; effortless means just enough effort to be vivid, to be present, to be here, to be now. To be bright. My teacher used to call this "effortless effort." We each need to find out for ourselves what this means. Too much effort and we get too tight; too little effort and we get dreamy. Somewhere in the middle is a state of vividness and clarity and inner brightness. This is what I mean when I suggest that people not make too much effort. You must find out for yourself how much that is.

Our Natural Tendency Is to Awaken

When we meditate in the way I am describing—when we let go of control and allow everything to be as it is—our natural tendency is to awaken. We are biologically and psychologically wired to move toward awakening. A lot of people don't know that. But when we let go of the control that the ego has, the nature of our being is to awaken.

Now, of course, people come to me from their own traditions of meditation, and when I suggest that they let go of their technique they often find that initially mind wanders a bit. This is natural. When we let go of something we've been holding very tightly, it tends to want to escape. It's like keeping your dog on a leash; when you take the leash off, the tendency of the dog is to run. It's the same for our minds. If we have leashed our minds tightly, when we let go of that leash the tendency of the mind is to run around. But just like letting a dog off leash, we can simply allow it to happen. Your dog may run away from you quickly, but if you hang out for a while, eventually your dog will usually decide it wants to wander back to your feet. In a similar way, when you let go of controlling your mind, it may be a little noisy for a while. But if you really let it be as it is, its tendency will be to return to a state of harmony, a state of quietness.

Let Everything Within You Reveal Itself to You

Since the nature of our entire being is to awaken, when we allow everything to be as it is in a deep way, what often happens is that repressed material within our psyche emerges. In fact, a lot of spiritual students unconsciously use their meditation techniques to keep repressed material repressed. They may not know that they are doing this, but this is what is happening. When we let go and really open and allow things to be as they are, it's not uncommon for certain repressed material to come up, which can be quite shocking. All of a sudden, you may have a fit of anger in your meditation or a fit of sadness. You may find yourself weeping. You may find various memories will come through your consciousness and reveal themselves. You might have physical pains; people report that various parts of their bodies become painful when they allow everything to be as it is. When we really start to let go, what needs to rise to the surface rises to the surface. The mind may not want this material to arise; as I said, many spiritual people unknowingly use their spiritual discipline to suppress their unconscious. When we stop suppressing, our unconscious starts to come up and reveal itself.

What do we do with this unconscious material that rises to the surface? Nothing. We simply allow it to reveal itself. It does not need to be analyzed. What arises is, for the most part, unresolved conflict within us: emotions we've never allowed ourselves to feel fully, experiences we've never allowed ourselves to experience fully, pains we've never allowed ourselves to feel fully. All of this arises. This unresolved material within us yearns to be experienced fully, without being relegated to unconsciousness. So when our repressed material arises, we need to allow it to arise without suppressing it. Without analyzing, we allow these feelings to be experienced in the body, in our being, and to unfold as they will. What you'll find if you do this is that whatever kind of pain it is—whether it's emotional, psychic, physical, spiritual, or otherwise—this repressed material will arise, reveal itself, be experienced, and then pass away. If it doesn't pass away, you will know that somewhere there is resistance, or denial, or indulgence—which is a good thing to recognize, because it gives you the opportunity to let go of it once again.

Now, just because we allow everything to be as it is doesn't mean that our meditation is necessarily going to stay totally peaceful and silent. The point here is awakening, right? The point is not to learn how to suppress yourself so that you feel better. It's how to wake up to the reality of your being, and we wake up to the reality of our being by relating with our human nature, not by avoiding it. Not by going around it. Not by trying to pray it away or mantra it away or meditate it away. We wake up by letting everything within ourselves reveal itself, be felt, be experienced, be known. Then and only then can we move on to a deeper level. This is very, very important and it's something a lot of people don't understand. It's easy to use meditative techniques to suppress our human experiences, to suppress things that we don't want to feel. But what is called for is just the opposite. True Meditation is the space in which everything gets revealed, everything gets seen, everything gets experienced. And as such, it lets go of itself. We don't even let go. It lets go of itself.

Fear Is Often a Doorway

I am frequently asked about fear. Fear is very often a part of the spiritual path. When people sit down and meditate it's not at all uncommon for fear to arise at some point. This is especially the case with this sort of meditation, in which we are endeavoring to actually let go of control and manipulation. In most human beings, this will give rise to a certain amount of fear, because the egoic mind is very, very afraid of letting go of control and experiencing openness. A lot of fear can arise with meditative self-inquiry as well—when we look within and see that we don't actually exist as separate entities.

When the mind makes contact with the unknown, something it doesn't understand, it very often goes into fear. We're often taught that if fear arises there must be some mistake being made, that fear must mean danger. But in spirituality it's important to remember that fear doesn't necessarily mean danger. Actually, fear often means that we're going to a much deeper place inside ourselves. So if fear arises, the wisest thing to do is simply to let it arise. Feel it in your body. Notice that your mind tends to create stories and ideas about the fear, and recognize that these stories aren't really true. But let the fear be experienced, because fear is often a doorway. It's something that you must walk through. When you are willing to walk through the fear, to experience it, to see what's underneath it, to go deeper, then fear has served its purpose. The arising of fear doesn't always mean that something has gone wrong. Actually, in spirituality, fear often means that something is beginning to go right.

Getting Out of Our Minds and into Our Senses

True Meditation is getting out of our minds and into our senses, actually feeling what it is we are feeling. We hear what is happening around us rather than just hearing our thoughts. We see what's in front of us rather than being totally occupied by the little movies in our minds. In True Meditation, we're in the body as a means to transcend it. It is paradoxical that the greatest doorway to the transcendence of form is through form itself. And so, when you sit down to meditate, connect with your senses—connect with how you feel, what you hear, what you sense, what you smell. Your senses actually anchor you in the moment. When your mind wanders, anchor yourself in your senses. Start to listen. What are the sounds outside? Start to feel. How do you feel in your body? Enter into the felt sense, the kinesthetic sense of your being. Connect not only with what you feel in your body, but also with what you sense in the room. Start to smell. As you are sitting, what does it smell like? Through your senses, open to the whole world within and around you. This grounds you in a deeper reality than your mind, and it also helps focus you in a place other than your mind. Allowing everything to be is extraordinarily simple, but it's not as easy as people imagine. If you're actually doing it correctly, you'll find yourself vividly present to your five senses, vividly present to your body, vividly present to your experience. If, on the other hand, you find that you're in a hazy dream zone, then it's very important to come back to your senses. Your body is a beautiful tool to anchor consciousness in a deeper sense of reality.

Awareness Is Dynamic

When we stop manipulating and controlling it, we discover that awareness itself is not fixed. When awareness is not directed, it may rest for a while. It may be globally aware, so that everything in your senses is being taken in all at once. Often, the more you relax, the more globally aware you become, feeling the totality of experience, taking in everything and all experience as a single whole. But then things might change. Awareness is curious by nature. You might have a tickle in your toe or a feeling in your side or a contraction somewhere, and awareness will naturally, spontaneously move in that certain direction. "Naturally" is the key word here; it will move not because you think it should, but because it has a natural way it wants to flow. Allowing everything to be as it is does not generate a static state. Awareness may go to your foot, to pain, or to tension. It may go to a sense of joy. It may hear a bird outside and it might just spontaneously listen to the bird, then it may become global and take in everything all at once. Awareness may suddenly become curious about silence itself and enter into silence. Allowing everything to be as it is actually generates a much more dynamic inner environment than the words suggest. You have to discover within yourself what this actually means.

What you will find is that awareness is very dynamic; it has a tendency to move around. Sometimes awareness will stop and rest in a deep sense of silence and stillness. By letting go, we allow awareness to do what it wants to do. It goes where it needs to go. We realize that awareness has an intelligence in and of itself. The invitation for you as a meditator is to become very engaged with where awareness wants to go, with what it wants to experience, with what it wants to look at. You are engaged; you're right with it. You are willing to go where awareness wants to go.

Live in the Same Way You Meditate

Sitting meditation is a beautiful thing for people to do. In my experience, most people would do well to spend some time sitting in silence every day, whether it's twenty minutes or forty-five minutes. If you are drawn to more, then do more. You may be drawn to an hour a day; you may be drawn to two hours a day. Again, it's really connecting with what you're drawn to do. Not what your mind is drawn to do, but what your heart is drawn to do.

But when I talk about meditation, I am not simply talking about something we do when we're sitting down in a formal way. Meditation also has to do with life and living. If we only learn how to meditate well when we are sitting down, as profound as that may be, it doesn't go far enough. Even if you sit three hours a day, that still leaves twenty-one hours a day when you are not sitting. And if you sit for two minutes a day, that leaves an awful lot of time when you are not sitting.

What I have found over the years is that even really good meditators leave their meditation behind when they get off the cushion. While they're meditating, they can let go of their ideas, their beliefs, their opinions, and their judgments. They can let it all go, and they can meditate very well. But once they are off the cushion, they somehow feel like they need to pick it all back up again. True Meditation is something that actually lives with us. We can do it anytime, anyplace, and anywhere. You can be driving down the street in your car and allowing everything to be as it is. You can have the practice of allowing the traffic to be as it is. You can have the practice of letting yourself feel as you feel. You can let the weather be as it is. Or the next time you meet your friend or your lover, you can investigate the experience. What is it like to meet this person when I allow them to be as they are completely? What is it like when I allow me to be as I am completely? What happens? How do we engage? How does it change? So True Meditation can be a very active meditation, a very engaged meditation.

In fact, it's important that meditation is not seen as something that only happens when you are seated in a quiet place. Otherwise spirituality and our daily life become two separate things. That's the primary illusion—that there is something called "my spiritual life," and something called "my daily life." When we wake up to reality, we find they are all one thing. It's all one seamless expression of spirit.

What if the foundation of your life, and not just the foundation of your time spent in meditation, became allowing everything to be as it is? This would be a revolutionary foundation for most people's lives. It is revolutionary to have the foundation of your existence, the bottom line of your existence, be allowing everything to be as it already is. This means allowing everything to be as it was, and as it is now, and as it might be. What if the foundation of your life itself, all those other hours in the day when you aren't sitting in silence, were occupied by allowing everything to be as it is?

If you did this, your life might become quite interesting. Because meditation is safe. You go onto your little cushion, you sit on your little chair or your little bench, you curl up in whatever posture you like. Right? It's safe; it's like going back into the womb. Which is wonderful because it is nice to discover a safe place, a place within yourself that is entirely dependable, a place within yourself that nothing and nobody can take away. That's really nice. But when we start to open up and think of meditation not simply as being in a safe place but as an approach to life itself, it gets very interesting, doesn't it? We begin to come out of resistance to experience. And when we start to come out of resistance to experience, we start to discover something that is very potent and very powerful.

We begin to discover the most essential thing, which is the truth of our being. We begin to discover that our essential nature as consciousness is always allowing everything to be as it is. That's why we meditate in this way, because that's what consciousness is already doing—it's allowing everything to be as it is. Consciousness itself is not in resistance. Consciousness is not in opposition to what is. Have you noticed this? Consciousness, or your true nature, is allowing everything to be as it is. If you are having a good day, your true nature allows you to have a good day. And if you are having a rotten day, your true nature doesn't get in the way of you having a rotten day either. Right? It allows it to be as it is. That's not the only thing our consciousness is doing, but it's the foundation.

I have found that one of the keys to really being free is to live in the same way as you meditate. When we really allow everything to be as it is, in that inner atmosphere, in that inner attitude of non-grasping, that's a very fertile space—a very potent state of consciousness. In those moments of surrender, something creative can come to you. That is the space in which insight arises, in which revelation arises. So it's not that we just let everything be as it is as a goal, as an endpoint. If you make it a goal, you miss the point. The point isn't simply to allow everything to be as it is; that's just the base, the underlying attitude. From that underlying attitude, lots of things become possible. That's the space in which wisdom arises, in which "Ahas" arise. It's the space in which we are gifted with what we need to see. It's the space in which we can be informed by the wholeness of consciousness, not just by a little speck of consciousness in our mind. And ultimately, it is the space in which realization arises. It is the space in which we realize ourselves to be consciousness itself, the unmanifest fabric of being.

PART TWO

Meditative Self-Inquiry

Once we have laid the foundation of allowing everything to be as it is in the deepest and simplest way, and we have some taste of what that experience is like, then the next element of meditation really comes into play. This element is meditative self-inquiry. It is a part of meditation that is often overlooked, and yet it is very important.

If we just left meditation at allowing everything to be as it is in a deep way, as profound as that is and as freeing as that can be, that approach on its own could lead us into a state of spiritual dryness or inner disengagement. Inquiry is a way in which we use the energy of our natural curiosity, the energy of spiritual yearning itself, to cultivate radical insight into the nature of our own being.

How I Discovered Meditative Self-Inquiry

I like to tell the story of how I came across meditative self-inquiry. In many ways, it was very spontaneous, almost a mistake. Nobody ever taught me about meditative self-inquiry directly, and nobody even suggested that I do it. It came naturally out of years of spiritual practice and meditating.

At one point, I realized that I had these question—questions I think lots of people have about their practice, about their spirituality, about life. My questions were actually fairly basic. For example, what is surrender? I had heard a lot about surrender, and I thought, what is surrender, really? And what is meditation? What is it really? I had been meditating for years, but what was it really? This line of questioning ultimately led me to ask, who am *I* really? I noticed that these questions were running around in my mind, and I was looking for a way in which I could actually engage with them directly. And that's how I discovered meditative self-inquiry.

I found myself going to coffee shops in the evenings after work, and I would start with a question. I would take a piece of paper and a pen in hand and I would start to write about the question as if I was talking to somebody else. We are always the best in transmitting what we know when we are teaching it to somebody else, so I would sit down and write as if I were teaching the answer to someone. The agreement I made with myself was that I was not going to write a single word unless I knew in my experience that it was accurate and true. So I would take a topic like "what is surrender?" And I would start to write on it. As I said, I would not complete a sentence until I felt that that sentence was true, that I wasn't in any way speaking outside of my own experience. In this way, I would write the next sentence, and the next sentence, and the next sentence. What I found was that I would write myself right up to the end of my knowledge about the subject I was investigating in a relatively short period of time. I found that usually within two handwritten pages, three at the very most, I would write myself right up to the edge of what I knew. And so I would come up to this inner wall, and I would feel it—not only in my mind, but in my body too. I would know: this is it; this is as far as my own experience goes.

I could sense that I had not gotten to the bottom of what my question was, so I would literally sit there with my pen in one hand, and a cup of coffee in the other hand, and I would refuse to write a word unless I knew that it was true. Sometimes I would sit right at that place for many minutes, sometimes half an hour, sometimes two hours—but I would not write the next word until I knew that it was true and it was accurate. What I found was that the only way to move was to hold still, right there at the edge of my knowledge, and feel into my mind and my body at that threshold.

Not to think about the question. Not to go into a lot of philosophizing in my mind. But literally to kinesthetically hold at that boundary between what I knew and what was beyond what I knew. And what I found was that by holding at that boundary—by feeling it, by sensing it, by knowing that I wanted to move beyond it—that eventually the next word or sentence would come. When it did, I would write it down. Sometimes I would write no more than half a sentence before I would know, right in the middle, that I had hit the boundary again. I would stop again and I would wait. I'd hold at the boundary.

Eventually I found that I could go through this mysterious limitation, this mysterious wall of what I knew, and I could move beyond it. And I knew when I had moved beyond it, because all of a sudden everything would start to flow again. I would start to write things that I never knew that I knew. All of a sudden this deeper wisdom would come out, and I would be writing it down, and eventually I would reach a conclusion.

Now these writings were not very long. I think the longest I ever wrote was probably seven or eight handwritten pages. So they weren't long dissertations; I was trying to make them the shortest, most succinct expressions of what I knew. And when I was finished writing, what I found, number one and most important, was that the question had disappeared. And number two, the answer to every question was ultimately the same answer. It is the answer that each of us has to come to for ourselves, the answer that each one of us needs to discover through our own process of self-inquiry. That answer is simply, "I am." What is surrender? "I am surrender." Surrender isn't something I do, surrender isn't an act that I perform. Surrender is an expression of my own truest being. No matter what question, I found that by the very end of it, I got to the same place—not to an answer in the mind, but to a living sense that it all ended in "I am."

I can't explain it intellectually, but it was a revelation that everything ended in the same place. So that was really how I came upon this form of inquiry. Once I realized how to do it through writing, I realized I could do the same sort of investigation without writing it down. Writing it down has a certain practical value, because it shows you what you know. You don't have to keep spinning in your mind. But later I found that I could do this process without writing it down, and that formed the basis of how I teach meditative self-inquiry today. In fact, sometimes I do suggest that people do this as a written practice if they are drawn to it. For others, it's not necessary to write it down. But it is necessary that you inquire with energy and focus and sincerity. We really have to want to know in order to do this effectively. Inquiry is not a plaything. We really have to want to know.

What Is a Spiritually Powerful Question?

Meditative self-inquiry is the art of asking a spiritually powerful question. And a question that is spiritually powerful always points us back to ourselves. Because the most important thing that leads to spiritual awakening is to discover who and what we are—to wake up from this dream state, this trance state of identification with ego. And for this awakening to occur, there needs to be some transformative energy that can flash into consciousness. It needs to be an energy that is actually powerful enough to awaken consciousness out of its trance of separateness into the truth of our being. Inquiry is an active engagement with our own experience that can cultivate this flash of spiritual insight.

I want to reiterate that, without inquiry, meditation can lead to a sort of inner disengagement. It can also lead to various meditative states, and entering meditative states is not the same as spiritual awakening. We use inquiry to break free of meditative states and to break free of all the other states that we walk around in as human beings—states which our minds become attached to and identify with.

As I said, the most important thing in spiritual inquiry is to ask the right question. The right question is a question that genuinely has energy for you. In spirituality, the most important thing initially, is to ask yourself, *what is the most important thing?* What is spirituality about for you? What is the question that's in your deepest heart? Not the question that someone tells you should be there, not what you've learned it should be. But what is the question *for you*? If you meditate, why are you doing it? What question are you trying to answer?

When you know what that question is, truly and authentically, then you can begin the process of self-inquiry. You can ask yourself that question in a quiet, meditative way and see where it leads you.

What or Who Am I?

In my own life, what I am primarily interested in is waking up from the dream state of identification to the truth of oneness. As a spiritual teacher, that's what all my teaching is centered around. So I suggest that people use meditative self-inquiry as a tool to help cultivate the energy of awakening, the awareness of one's true nature. However, many people I meet are actually looking outside of themselves and asking questions that are outside of their own experience. Everybody has heard the teaching "look within," and yet many of us are still looking outside of ourselves. Even when we have spiritual questions, they are often focused outside of ourselves. What is God? What is the meaning of life? Why am I here? These are questions that may be relevant to the personality, but they are still not the most intimate question.

The most intimate question we can ask, and the one that has the most spiritual power, is this: What or who am I? Before I wonder why I am here, maybe I should find out who this "I" is who is asking the question. Before I ask "What is God," maybe I should ask who I am, this "I" who is seeking God. Who am I, who is actually living this life? Who is right here, right now? Who is on the spiritual path? Who is it that is meditating? Who am I really? It is this question which begins the journey of spiritual self-inquiry, finding out, for your own self, who and what you truly are.

So step number one is having a spiritually powerful question, such as "Who or what am I?" Step number two is knowing how to ask that question. Again, I have noticed that very few people know how to ask a spiritually powerful question. If we don't know how to ask, then we'll just end up lost in our minds. We can sit around thinking forever about who we are. We can read spiritual discourses, philosophical discourses, religious discourses on who we are and why we are here and what this is all about. We can do that forever, and what we end up with is more thoughts, more ideas, more beliefs—not what we really need, which is a flash of insight, a flash of recognition into the truth of our being. Spiritual inquiry actually helps cultivate that flash. So how do we ask the question? How do we find out what we truly are?

The Way of Subtraction

Before we actually find out what we are, we must first find out what we are not. Otherwise our assumptions will continue to contaminate the whole investigation. We could call this the way of subtraction. In the Christian tradition, they call this the Via Negativa, the negative path. In the Hindu tradition of Vedanta, they call this Neti-neti, which means "not this, not that." These are all paths of subtraction, ways of finding out what we are by finding out what we are not.

We start by looking at the assumptions we have about who we are. We all have many, many assumptions that we don't even realize we have. And so we start to look at the simplest things about ourselves. For example, we look at our minds and we notice that there are thoughts. Clearly there is something or someone that is noticing the thoughts. You may not know what it is, but you know it's there. Thoughts come and go, but that which is witnessing the thoughts remains.

If thoughts come and go, then they aren't really what you are. Starting to realize that you are not your thoughts is very significant, since most people assume they are what they think. They believe they are their thoughts. Yet a simple look into your own experience reveals that you are the *witness* of your thoughts. Whatever thoughts you have about yourself aren't who and what you are. There is something more primary that is watching the thoughts.

In the same way, there are feelings. We all have emotional feelings: happiness, sadness, anxiety, joy, peace. We have feelings in the body, be they feelings of energy—a contraction here, an openness there—or just an itch on your toe. There are various feelings, and then there is the witness of those feelings. Something is witnessing or taking note of every feeling you have. So you have feelings, and you have the awareness of feelings. Feelings come and go, but the awareness of feelings remains. And although we need not deny any feeling we experience, it is important to notice that our deepest and truest identity is not a feeling. It cannot be, because there is something more primary before feelings arise: awareness of feelings.

The same is true for beliefs. We have many beliefs, and we have the awareness of those beliefs. They may be spiritual beliefs, beliefs about your neighbor, beliefs about your parents, beliefs about yourself (which are usually the most damaging), beliefs about a whole variety of things. Beliefs are thoughts that we assume to be true. We can all see that our beliefs have changed as we've grown, as we move through a lifetime. Beliefs come and go, but the awareness of beliefs stands before the beliefs; it is more primary. It is easy to see, then, that we cannot be our beliefs. Beliefs are something we witness, something we watch, something we notice. But beliefs do not tell us who the watcher is; they do not tell us who the noticer is. The watcher or the noticer, the witness, stands before the beliefs.

The same thing goes for our ego-personality. Everybody has an ego, and everybody has a personality. We tend to think that we are our egos, that we are our personalities. And yet, just as with thoughts, feelings, and beliefs, we can come to see that there is a witness to our ego-personality. There's an ego-personality called "you" and then there is a watching of the ego-personality, an awareness of the ego-personality. The awareness of the ego-personality stands before the personality; it is noticing it, without judging, without condemning.

Here we've started to move into something more intimate. Most people believe they are their egos and their personalities. But a simple willingness to look into your experience reveals that there is personality, and then there is the witness of personality. Therefore your essential, deepest nature cannot be your personality. Your ego-personality is being watched by something more primary; it is being witnessed by awareness.

With that, we arrive at awareness itself. We notice that there is awareness. Everybody has awareness. If you are reading these words right now, it is awareness that is actually taking this in. You are aware of what you think. You are aware of how you feel. So awareness is clearly present. It is not something that needs to be cultivated. Awareness is not something that needs to be manufactured. Awareness simply is. It is that which makes it possible to know, to experience what is happening.

Who Is Aware?

Generally we think, unconsciously, that "I am aware," that I am the one that is awareness, that awareness is something that belongs to me. We presume there is some entity called "me" who is aware. Yet when we start to investigate this meditatively, quietly, simply, we start to see that while there is awareness, we can't actually find the "I" or the "me" who is aware. We start to see that this is an assumption that the mind has been taught to make, that "I" am the one who is aware. When you turn inside and look for who's aware, what is aware, you can't find an "it." There's just more awareness. There isn't a "me" or an "I" who is aware.

In this way we are still subtracting our identity through this deep investigation. Through looking at what we are not, we are actually pulling our identity out of thought, feeling, persona, ego, body, mind. We are pulling our identity back out of the exterior elements of our experience into its essential nature. No sooner do we get back to awareness itself than we encounter the primary assumption that "I am the one who is aware." So we investigate that assumption. As we investigate it, through our experience, we discover time and time again that we cannot find out who it is that is aware. Where is this "I" that is aware? It is at this precise moment—the moment when we realize that we cannot find an entity called "me" who owns or possesses awareness—that it starts to dawn on us that maybe we ourselves are awareness itself. Awareness isn't something we own; awareness isn't something we possess. Awareness is actually what we are.

Now for some people—for most people—this will sound radical. This is because we are so used to identifying ourselves with our thoughts, with our feelings, with our beliefs, with our egos, with our bodies, and with our minds. We are actually *taught* to identify with these things. Yet through our investigation we start to see that something stands before thought, before personality, before beliefs—something that we are calling awareness itself. It can flash upon us through this investigation that we are awareness itself.

This does not mean that there are not thoughts. It doesn't mean that there's not a body. We're not in denial of ego or personality or belief or anything else. This is not a denial of all these exterior elements of our human self. We're simply discovering our essential nature. Bodies and minds and beliefs and feelings are like clothing that awareness puts on, and we are finding out what is underneath this clothing. It can be quite transformative to realize that you are not what you thought you were, that you are not your beliefs, that you are not your personality, that you are not your ego. You are something other than that, something that resides on the inside, at the innermost core of your being. For the moment we are calling that something "awareness" itself. The radical nature of this insight is not that awareness is something you possess, or that you need discipline or need to learn how to do. Awareness is actually what you are; it's the essence of your being. And not only is awareness what *you* are, it is also what everyone else is, too.

A Transcendent Recognition

This self-recognition can't be understood in the mind. It's a leap that the mind can't make. The mind may accept or deny that you are awareness, but either way it can't really understand. It cannot comprehend. Thought cannot comprehend what is beyond thought. That's why we call this a transcendent recognition, a transcendent revelation. It's actually our identity waking up from the prison of separation to its true state. This is both simple and extraordinarily profound. For some people it may come as a very quick flash, almost like a flash of lightning, where it is suddenly recognized that you are this awareness that's been watching from the inside all along. It may come as this sort of flash, and it may be gone just as quickly. Or it may flash upon you and last for a longer period of time. For others, it may flash and take hold, allowing them to realize their true nature indefinitely. No matter how it comes, it is very important to realize that this is not something that the mind decides on. It is a flash of revelation.

One of the simplest pointers I can give is to remember that this process of subtraction, this process of inquiry and investigation, really takes place from the neck down. We may ask the question—"What am I?" or "Who am I?" or "Am I this thought?"—and the question, of course, originates in the mind. But once we've asked the question, it's very important that we don't stay in the mind. We must turn our attention to the neck down. We have this whole beautiful thing called a body and this kinesthetic sense of being, and that's where inquiry really happens.

An example of this is when you ask yourself, "What am I?" The first thing most people realize is that they don't know. They don't actually know who or what they are. So most people will go into their minds to try to figure it out. But the first thing that your mind knows is that you don't know. In spiritual inquiry that's very useful information. "I don't know what I am. I don't know who I am." Once you recognize that, you can either think about it or you can actually feel it. What is it like to feel in your being that you don't know what you are? What's it like when you look inside to find out who you are and you don't find an entity called "you"? What does that open space feel like? Feel it in your body; let it register in the cells of your being. This is real spiritual inquiry. This transforms what might have been just an abstract thought in the mind into something that is very visceral, very kinesthetic, and very spiritually powerful.

Natural Harmony

As I said before, it is important to realize that although we are taking back or extracting our identity out of thought and feeling and personality, we are not denying or dissociating ourselves from these exterior elements of experience. Inquiry is not a practice of pushing anything away; it is simply a way of getting identity to wake up from the dream of separation. But even when it wakes up, there is still a body there. There is still a personality there. There is still a rudimentary ego structure there. The difference is that once we recognize ourselves as awareness itself, our identity can begin to rest in its essence. Who we are is no longer found in our body, mind, personalities, thoughts, and beliefs. Who we are rests in its source.

When we rest in our source, our bodies and minds and personalities and feelings come into harmony. What I mean by harmony is that we are no longer divided against ourselves. I think most human beings can recognize that often the ego is actually defined by a certain inner divisiveness; certain parts of our egos are at war or are at odds with other parts of our egos. We want to be somebody that we can't really be. We want to think thoughts that we can't really think. We want to appear in ways that we don't actually appear. We want to be better than we actually are. We have all these conflicting ideas and feelings and emotions when our identity is caught up in ego-personality.

Quite mysteriously, when we extract our identity from the ego-personality, the ego-personality comes into a harmony. These psychic and emotional forces are no longer at odds with each other. This harmony may not immediately arise in its deepest possible way, but this is where the journey begins. We come into a harmony of body, mind, and personality because we are no longer identified with body, mind, and personality.

The Great Inclusion

Self-inquiry begins with finding out who we are not, but this is not where self-inquiry ends. After the Way of Subtraction comes what I call the Great Inclusion.

After we have pulled our identity out of thought and belief and personality and ego and seen that there is something more primary, identity starts to rest in awareness itself. Of course, we should not let the mind fixate on an idea that says, "I am awareness." That idea may be useful, but that idea also is a limiting fixation. Of course, it's much more freeing to identify yourself as awareness than to identify yourself as a thought form or an ego or a personality. It's also freeing to see that everybody else is awareness, too. But we should not get stuck in a new concept, in a new way of identifying ourselves. "Awareness" is just a word. Another word for awareness could be spirit. Awareness (or spirit) is something that has no form, no shape, no color, no gender, no age, no beliefs. It is transcendent of all that. Awareness or spirit simply means a beingness, a sense of aliveness which transcends all of our form.

I'm using this concept of "awareness" interchangeably with the concept of "spirit." If you look within, you can notice for yourself in this moment that awareness (or spirit) is not resisting thought. There is thought, but awareness is not resisting thought. There is feeling, but awareness is not resisting feeling. There is an ego-personality, but awareness is not resisting the ego-personality. Awareness is not trying to change things; awareness is not trying to fix anything. You can start to notice that there is this presence of awareness within you, which is not trying to change your humanness. It's not trying to alter you. Just as important, it's not trying to alter others. This awareness is totally inclusive. It is a state of being where everything is okay simply the way it is.

Paradoxically, the ego-personality always needs to experience this state of not needing itself to be fixed in order to come into harmony and peace. The ego-personality always needs to come into a direct experiential contact with a presence that is not trying to change it. It's amazing for a human being to realize his or her true nature is not trying to change their human nature. This allows the human nature to rest, to no longer feel separate from its source. We start to feel unity within ourselves. We stop feeling that we are divided within ourselves, because we see that ultimately there is no dividing line between awareness, or spirit, and our ego-personality. There's really no separation between the two.

When we start to let go into awareness or spirit, we start to recognize that *that is* who and what we are. We start to see that everything in existence is simply a manifestation of spirit. Everything is an expression of spirit, whether it's the chair you are sitting on or the floor you are lying on or the shoes you wear. Everything is an expression of spirit:

the trees outside, the sky, everything. In the same way, the body that you call "you," the mind, the ego, the personality—all are expressions of spirit.

When our identification is caught in these various forms, the result is suffering. But when, through inquiry and meditation, our identity starts to come back to its home ground of awareness, then everything is included. Everything starts to be seen as a manifestation of spirit, including your humanness, with all of its strengths and weaknesses and all of its funny little quirks. You discover that your humanness is in no way separate from the divinity within you, which is what you actually are. I call this the Great Inclusion because we start to realize that our truest nature includes our whole human experience, that our human body, mind, and personality are nothing but an extension of spirit. It's the way spirit moves in the world of time and space. That's what a human body-mind is: an extension of spirit in time and space.

Now please don't try to understand this with your mind. This is really not understandable in the mind. This knowing resides at a deeper point, at a deeper place within ourselves. Something else understands; something else knows.

Notice What About You Remains the Same

For some people this recognition that we are awareness itself may seem quite abstract. For those who have realized it, it's not abstract at all. It is their living experience. If it feels abstract to you, I can suggest something very simple: try to notice what about you has always been there, throughout your lifespan. No matter how old or young you are, notice that throughout your life things have changed: your body has changed, your mind has changed, your ego has changed, your beliefs have changed, your personality has changed. All of it has been in a state of flux over many years. But all along, from the time you attained language, you always referred back to yourself as "I": "I am this. I think that. I believe this. I believe that. I want this. I want that." While everything else has changed and continues to change, the "I" that you refer to has always been there. When you say "I," it is the same "I" now as when you were a little child. The exteriors have changed. The thoughts have changed. The body has changed. The feelings have changed. But the "I" has not. On the level of intuition, there is a knowing that remains the same as it ever was, and you refer to it every time you say "I." Without you even recognizing it, that's the part of you that's divine. That's the sacred part. That's your essential nature. But that "I" has no form and no shape. It is of the nature of awareness and spirit. And so anybody can notice for themselves and within themselves that this sense of "I" has been there all along.

But this "I" is not what the mind thinks it is. Meditative self-inquiry allows you to discover for yourself who and what this "I" really is. I call it "meditative self-inquiry" because it is very experiential. It is not philosophical. It is not intellectual. Here, "meditative" means "experiential." Inquiry is only powerful when it is meditative, when we are looking in a sustained and focused and quiet way into our own experience.

Nobody can force this flash of recognition into being. It happens spontaneously. It happens by itself. But what we can do is cultivate the ground and create the conditions under which this flash of recognition happens. We can open our minds to deeper possibilities and start to investigate for ourselves what we really and truly are.

When this awakening to our true nature happens, it may happen for a moment, or it may happen for a longer period of time, or it may happen permanently. Whichever way it occurs, it is perfectly okay. Who you are is who you are. You cannot lose who you are, no matter what your experience is. Even if you have a certain opening and you realize your true nature, and then later you think you've forgotten it, you haven't lost anything. Therefore the invitation is always to rest more and more deeply, to not grasp at an insight or an experience, to not try and hold on to it, but to recognize the underlying reality, that which never changes. The great twentieth-century Indian sage Ramana Maharshi had a saying, "Let what comes come; let what goes go. Find out what remains." Meditative self-inquiry is a way of finding out what remains, what has always been.

Into the Mystery

It's not necessary to sit in a formal way to engage in meditative self-inquiry. You can ask the question "What am I?" anywhere, at any time. You can ask, "What is it that is driving the car? What is it that is drinking this tea? What is it that is reading these words?" It is a very simple question: "What am I? What am I outside of a thought or a memory? What am I behind all that?" When the mind asks the question, the mind looks within. And what does the mind find? It doesn't find anything. It doesn't find a new somebody because a new somebody would just be another thought or another image. So the mind looks within and says honestly, "I don't know." And this is a very mysterious moment for the mind. At this moment, you are actually in a state of unknowing. You are connected with the mystery of you, rather than the idea of you. Meditative self-inquiry can be an extraordinarily rapid, almost instantaneous introduction to the mystery of you. It returns you to the unknown very quickly and very efficiently. Once you get there, you can stay there and stay there—you can sense the unknown, kinesthetically feel the unknown, stay with the presence of what is unknown. In this way, meditative self-inquiry brings you very quickly to openness, to a big awake space. And, of course, spiritual realization is the realization that you *are* that space.

Beginning the True Spiritual Journey

The beginning of the spiritual journey is what I call "life after awakening." Instead of a life lived from a separate ego, from the illusion of the egoic personality, it is a life lived from the conscious recognition of our true nature as awareness. And that's truly a new life. It's a beginning. It's an end of the identification with thoughts, feelings, and the egoic personality, but—contrary to what some people think—it's not the end of spirituality. It's actually the beginning of the true spiritual journey, the beginning of a new way of life. It's the beginning of an ongoing discovery of what it's like to live from the recognition that you are spirit appearing as a human being.

This is the core of spirituality: awakening to who and what you are. In my experience of working with many people over the years, I have found two elements to be the most helpful and most powerful when it comes to awakening. The first is developing a meditative attitude, in which we let go of control on a very deep level and allow everything to be as it is. The second is a serious engagement with our own inherent curiosity and intelligence through meditative self-inquiry. Either one of these two separated can be incomplete: inquiry separated from meditation can become intellectual and abstract; meditation separated from inquiry can result in our getting lost in various different spiritual states. Combined, they provide the necessary energy, the necessary impetus, to produce a flash of recognition of your true nature. And in the end, that is what spirituality is all about.

An Interview with Adyashanti

The following interview took place after I attended my first five-day retreat with Adyashanti during which I was introduced to his radical approach to meditation.

Tami Simon: Adya, you were a Zen practitioner for fifteen years, and you compare the meditation practices that you did, sitting in zazen and meditating for long hours, to banging your head against a wall. But what if the Zen meditation that you did actually energetically prepared you for awakening and provided you with the insights that you now teach? Don't you think that's possible?

Adya: It's possible. Anything's possible. However, in my experience, what Zen practice really did for me was provide the avenue through which I eventually failed. It was my avenue for failure. The cushion was the place where I went to spiritual war with myself. I was trying to become enlightened and the cushion was where my own personal willfulness was playing itself out. In that sense, I can look back and say that it was necessary for me to engage in that battle with such intensity so that I could fail at it. I found out once and for all that I wasn't going to win the spiritual battle, and I finally let it go. So in that sense, those years of Zen practice were quite useful. But I think it would be very misleading to say that therefore everybody needs to go that route. I think we all go whatever route we go.

TS: Your Zen teacher was Arvis Justi. I've never heard of her.

Adya: Almost nobody has actually. She trained with quite a number of the early Zen masters who came from Japan to America in the last century, primarily Yasutani

Roshi and Maezumi Roshi. And many really excellent teachers were part of this first wave of Zen masters who came to America because Zen in Japan had become very traditional, very institutionalized. People would go to their Zen temple in the way that some people—not all—go to church. You know, "It's Sunday, let's go to the Zen temple and meditate." So these early Zen teachers who came to America were looking for fresh blood; they were looking for some very sincere people. And, of course, when we're actually awakened and we're called to teach, that's what we want: to teach people who are really sincere.

At that time, there were almost no Zen temples in America. So something like forty people would pack my teacher's house in Northern California in order to practice. People would sleep on the lawn and all over the place. After a while, my teacher's teacher said to her, "You don't need me to come up here, you teach this now." And that was it. There wasn't any kind of traditional dharma ceremony. And my teacher was very clear. She didn't feel she was cut out to be a priest. She was an older woman by this time, she had raised five kids, and she realized that although Zen can take a traditional path, she'd seen that that wasn't necessary and she wasn't drawn to that.

She taught in her house, and she never advertised. In the beginning, she would set up cushions in her living room every Sunday morning and sit, and nobody showed up for a year and a half. And every week she'd put the cushions out and she'd have a talk ready. She would just sit down and nobody would show up. Of course, who's going to show up when you're not advertising? But she just kept at it with this absolute dedication. And after a year and a half, one person showed up. And so she sat with that one person every weekend for a year. And then another person showed up, and so it went. She never sought to be known and she never really even saw herself as a teacher. She was a very unassuming person.

At that time, Zen was starting to become known in America and people like me were attracted to the robes and the temples and the ceremonies and stuff. And here's this little old lady who welcomes you into her house through the back door and she's wearing normal clothes and you go in her living room and you sit down. And from the exterior, it wasn't impressive at all. In fact, I don't think I really understood what she was offering until she suggested that I go to a temple and do a long retreat, the first retreat I ever did. When I came back after that retreat, which was really quite rigorous, I was literally blown away. I thought, "My God, what's there is here, and even more so. In this little lady's living room and kitchen on Sunday mornings there is as much dharma and maybe more dharma than when I was up at the retreat." I can't really communicate it, but it was really quite shocking. She was so unassuming that I think the vast majority of people missed it. They missed her, they missed what she was, and they missed what she had to offer.

TS: Even though you teach in your own way based on your discoveries about True Meditation and your writing experiments, do you feel that you are part of a lineage? Do you feel that you are carrying her lineage?

Adya: I do very much, actually. She has such a deep place in my heart, and I feel very much like a part of her lineage.

She told a story about the first time she ever sat down to teach. Of course, nobody showed up. But she sat and continued to sit in her living room every Sunday morning. And somebody once told her, "Boy, that must have been lonely, that must have been difficult." And she said, "It wasn't." She said, "Every time I'd sit there I could feel and almost see all the lineage holders before me. I could feel that." And the first retreat that I ever taught as a teacher, I remember sitting down and having the exact same experience. I felt like I was the tip of the iceberg of this very, very long lineage of beings that had so compassionately done what they could to pass this on. So I do feel very much that I'm part of a lineage. I feel very intimately the transmission that I got from her, not simply the transmission of awakening, but the transmission of her incredible integrity as a human being. It almost feels like it got directly put into me in some energetic way. She just had so much integrity, and of course she had a lot of grace, too. There was no presentation; there was nothing phony about her in any way whatsoever. It took me a lot of years to see that it had slowly seeped into me, an appreciation for that integrity. I don't have a lot of grace like she had, but I can almost feel that there's a place in my body that feels like it's her integrity, that energetically feels like her. Probably more than anything, that's what she gave me.

TS: Do you have any concern that the path that actually took you to where you are is not the path that you're teaching?

Adya: No concern whatsoever. The path I am teaching is very much the path that brought me to where I am. When I lead a retreat, we always spend five or six periods a day in silent sitting. But I discovered that my spirituality really started to take off when I wasn't relying exclusively on meditation practice. Even though I kept meditating, there was a point where there was a fundamental shift and I was no longer relying entirely on the practice. I could see that meditation in and of itself wasn't working for me. I didn't totally reject it, but this other element started to come in, which was inquiry. I started to fundamentally question everything. I started to look at things very deeply, very intently.

And then of course, the awakening part is always spontaneous. There are no ABCs of how to wake up. But when I look back, I saw these two things: stillness and silence, and the ability to be ruthlessly honest with myself, to not fool myself, to not tell myself that I knew something that I didn't, to stay with my line of inquiry. After a while, these two approaches together became my spiritual path. And these two things combined are what I teach.

TS: In that sense, are you teaching a path?

Adya: Sure. A pathless path [laughs]. But yes, you could say it's a path. It's not a path like "one plus two equals three," and it's not a path like "just keep walking and you end up at the top of the mountain." It's not a path in that sense. It's not a path that particularly has the feeling of progression. It's a way of being with experience. It's a way of being with yourself that actually unhinges the personal self. Whether you know it or not, whether you're conscious of it or not, the path is actually deconstructing you. Silence deconstructs you, but for most people silence isn't enough. Just meditating isn't enough. There's also this more active part of deconstruction, which is direct questioning and inquiry.

TS: In your retreats, you often suggest that people inquire using the question "What am I?" I've never heard that suggestion before. Most people who teach self-inquiry suggest that students work with the question "Who am I?"

Adya: "Who am I?" never worked for me. Even though for some people it works well, for me "Who am I?" implies an entity. "What am I?" feels to me like a more open-ended question.

TS: And you don't care if people come to your retreats and slouch during the silent sitting periods? I'm curious about that because it goes against a lot of the training that I've had.

Adya: It goes against a lot of the training that I've had, too.

TS: So why don't you care about that? Don't we want to sit in such a way that we are open and alert and the energetic pathways of the body can flow freely?

Adya: No, actually. [Laughs.] I say that because I've seen many people wake up while slouching. [Laughs.] And I always use what I observe, what my direct experience is. Do you have to be sitting in the lotus position, does your spine have to be straight in order for awakening to occur? No. Simply through observation, simply through watching what actually happens rather than listening to what any tradition has said, it's become clear to me that none of that has to happen for awakening. Is sitting with an erect posture useful for some things? Of course it's useful for some things. It can open up certain pathways, as you mentioned, and there are certain postures that are themselves more open postures. Of course that's true. But what I found through my Zen background was that a lot of people were so intense about correct posture that even though they sat in a very open posture—a lotus posture with the hands in the correct mudra—even though everything was externally right, their internal attitude was actually very tight and very closed. What I've seen is that it is the attitude that is important. If the attitude and the posture are one, then it's working. But so often, when posture is overemphasized, the posture may be right but the attitude is not open. And it is the internal attitude that has all the power. There's a teaching that if you have the right posture, the attitude will follow, and that's just not so. At least not for most people.

TS: Many meditation teachers work with beginning students by teaching some kind of concentration practice. Then, once people are familiar with basic concentration practices, they have the opportunity to loosen up a bit and explore. I believe many meditation teachers begin with concentration training because they are concerned that otherwise students will spend their whole time spinning in thought instead of meditating.

Adya: Probably so.

TS: But you're not afraid that people are sitting around at your retreats lost in thought without having had that training?

Adya: What I've found is that many times people show up at retreats and either they haven't meditated or they have been part of a meditative tradition. Either way, it can take them a while to catch on to what I'm teaching. And of course, when people stop manipulating, a lot of times their mind does go kind of crazy for a period of time. Oftentimes people at retreats will come to me looking for some means to control their thoughts. What I've found is that the more they stick with not manipulating, eventually—which usually doesn't mean years or months—eventually things start to quiet down in a natural way. And, of course, people ask me, "Can I follow my mantra? Can I follow my breath?" And I say, sure, if you find that helpful go ahead. If that's working for you, go ahead and do it. Just move in the direction of less and less and less and less and less.

What I have found is that although in theory there's usually a concentration practice that you learn that you are later supposed to let go of, most people don't actually ever let go. If you train yourself in manipulating your experience for ten years, it's really a deep-seated groove in your consciousness. Letting go of that can really be quite difficult. In theory that's how it's supposed to work, but oftentimes that's not what actually happens.

I think sometimes people have a fear, and maybe even certain teachers have a fear—although I don't know this for sure—that if you really let people's minds go crazy for a while and if people really allow themselves not to manipulate their experience, that maybe their minds will never stop. Or maybe they'll get lost somewhere. But I've truly found over and over and over again that the natural state starts to come around. The Zen teacher Suzuki Roshi said that the best way to control a cow is to give it a very, very big field. Don't put the fences too close together. And in a sense, I think that's what I'm doing. Create a really big field and eventually the mind won't try to bust out. Again, it's a different process from what people are used to, but again and again, I find that people come to retreats and in a day or two or three or sometimes four, a sort of natural process of relaxation and stillness starts to happen.

TS: Aren't you concerned that instead of meditating, people might just be spinning and spacing out?

Adya: I'm not concerned. I guess I'm different from a lot of teachers in this way. I don't see myself in any way as anybody's schoolteacher or parent. I'm here to talk to people who are actually really sincere about awakening. If they don't have that sincerity already, then they are with the wrong guy. Because I'm not going to give sincerity to them, and I'm not going to invest much energy into trying to get them to pretend like they are sincere. I know that, in a lot of traditions, teachers try to make their students be sincere. And I'm not saying that's wrong in any way, but that just doesn't happen for me. My attitude is, if you are sincere, then your sincerity is going to be a really powerful force in your life. And if you're not sincere, all the posture and all the this and that are not really going to have much effect. So if you want to sit in a lawn chair and stare at the clouds all day long, that's your thing. You see what I mean? If that's what you want to do, then that's what you'll do. If you ask me, I won't pretend that it's sincere and I won't pretend that it's leading to awakening. But I'm not in the business of trying to change what people want. I'm here, and if you really want truth, then we have something to talk about. The sincerity is totally up to you. It's not up to me;

it's up to you. You are going to sink or swim with this stuff from your own sincerity. If you have it, good. And if you don't have it, I'm not going to rescue you. In that sense, I'm really out of the babysitting business.

TS: What would you say to someone who partially feels sincere in their quest for truth but partially feels insincere?

Adya: I think most people actually do feel that way when they get right down to it. They have that sense of division. Usually what I suggest is that they look inside themselves, and make a really deep inquiry, an open-ended inquiry, into what they really, really want. I tell them to make no assumptions about what they want. And I often say, don't make it about what you think you should want. Or what a teaching said you should want. Really look at what you really, really, really want.

This type of inquiry can only happen if there are no shoulds, if there are no preconceived ideas about what you should want. This is what I mean by integrity: the willingness to really find out for yourself. And what I've discovered is that if someone really looks and sticks with this investigation, looking into what they really, really want, it can bring them much more to a unified place. It naturally brings them there. And to me, this is much better than trying to get to a unified place through discipline. Because people hear that kind of teaching—you must want awakening more than you want anything else—and it's true, but you can't pretend your way there, you can't fake your way there. Because you can't fool your own emotional radar. And I think that a lot of people are actually doing that—they hear the teachings and then they pretend that they are in a place that they're not.

I go about teaching in a totally different way. Because I know that if people can look deep inside themselves, they are going to find that they really do want the real truth. I know that if they look inside deeply enough, that's what they'll find. Because that's the ground of their being. It's also the core of their ego. Even the ego, in its deepest place, wants the truth.

TS: What do you mean by that—the core of the ego wants the truth? I thought my ego wanted things like fame, power, money, domination.

Adya: It does. It also wants all that, but all that is actually rather surface. Those are surface wants, surface desires. Of course, egos want all that stuff. Of course they want that, but if you go deep enough into the egoic self, deep into its core, you actually meet the truth, you meet the divine. The spark of it is right in the core of the ego.

That's why a lot of the time what I do is give the ego lots of room. People will say to me, "I don't think I want the truth, I want to do this or have that." And I say, "Go for it, do it." And it's amazing what happens as soon as you tell somebody, "You can do what you want, you can want what you want, go ahead, I don't care, God doesn't care, nothing thinks you're wrong, nothing in all of the universe except a thought thinks you're wrong for wanting what you want. Now go ahead." It's amazing how sometimes when you give someone total permission, how something deeper comes out. All of a sudden they drop into, "Now that I actually feel that I can want anything I want, I guess I don't really want what I thought I wanted. Now that I have permission, now that it is okay with the universe and God and guru and the divine and everything, I'm not really sure that that's even what I truly want." Because a lot of these surface egoic wants are very much held in place by a sense that these wants are not okay. It's very adolescent. Adolescents want to dye their hair orange as long as it freaks out mom and dad. But if mom and dad are totally okay with orange hair, they're not going to dye their hair orange anymore, are they? There's no mystique to it, there's no allure. But before they find out that it's okay, it's just about the most important thing in the world.

I understand that my approach is completely backward from the way spirituality is often taught. My approach is to help people really connect with their own integrity, because it's only when people are in touch with their own integrity that real spiritual discoveries can be made. People can't get there if they are stuck in shoulds or shouldn'ts.

TS: Sometimes when I hear people talk about how their true nature is awareness itself, it can sound to me like empty rhetoric that is really a type of spiritual bypassing. I can tell that this person is seething with rage or a nervous wreck and yet they know what inquiry is supposed to lead to and they mouth the words.

Adya: That's one of the reasons I have people meditate. I think of it as truth time. If you sit quietly for a period of time, sooner or later your denial starts to break down because it just gets too painful to sit there and lie to yourself about what's happening. During our retreats, sooner or later people will come up and start talking about this fear that they've always had or this unresolved issue they've never looked at or the fact that they are still in a rage about something that happened twenty years ago. Just sitting in silence is enough. It starts to break people down after a while. And that's one of the reasons I teach inquiry *and* meditation. If people think they've woken up to their true nature yet they can't sit still without going crazy, then they aren't half as awake as they think they are. Meditation is like an oven that forces the truth out.

I often tell people that I'm not having them meditate just so they can become good at meditation. When you meditate and you're not manipulating—which is of course new to a lot of meditators—then quite naturally there is this kind of unloading and the truth itself can spontaneously arise. And often what is unloaded is a lot of repressed material that people have been using their spirituality to suppress. When you just sit and you're not manipulating then you actually start to see the things you need to see and experience the things you need to experience. Old experiences may arise that have been waiting there for thirty years just to be experienced, not to be figured out necessarily, or analyzed, but just to be experienced without going unconscious. And what I've found over time is that as this natural unloading happens, people then have the energy they need to go deeper.

TS: I've heard you say that you don't believe that awakening—defined as a fundamental shift of identity out of the personality and into awareness itself—is actually that rare. And that in fact this belief that awakening is rare is actually an obstacle to awakening. You don't think that awakening is rare?

Adya: No.

TS: Why is this belief an obstacle?

Adya: Because almost all of us feel like we're not the chosen ones. Most of us feel pretty ordinary when you get right down to it. If you have this unconscious or conscious belief that awakening is only for very extraordinary people, that totally contradicts our sense of ourselves. This idea may be the most powerful impediment to awakening. Our examples of awakening feed this. We have images of the awake being, and they are halo-enshrouded, with long hair, flowing gowns, and if they're doing anything in life they are always teaching, they always have disciples, they always have people following at their feet. These images are out there, and yet it's simply not so. It's very hard for our minds to get that enlightenment can look like your grandmother or your grocer. It doesn't need to look in any way extraordinary. Some enlightened beings are very charismatic. But you know what? Some unenlightened beings are very charismatic. But these images really get in the way. Awakening isn't about becoming extraordinary. If anything, it's about becoming ordinary. It's about becoming who we really, really are.

TS: I think one of the reasons some people believe that awakening is rare is because they have been practicing meditation for twenty or thirty years and they haven't made the kind of breakthrough discoveries that you describe for yourself, and so there is a certain grumpiness or cynicism and a belief that enlightenment must be only for the rare few. Otherwise, they'd have to believe that there was something wrong with them or that they were a failure in some way.

Adya: That's one place their mind could go.

TS: Or that the path that they're following isn't working.

Adya: Ah! That's a much more threatening idea. Of course that's what I think contributed to my own awakening. I didn't blame it on the path but on my relationship with the path. That's why I encourage people to shake it up, shake it loose, let yourself question, open it up a bit. Don't be afraid to question. Look at yourself and see what hasn't worked. And have the courage to change, to move on if something's not working. Look with innocent eyes, very innocent, very open. That innocence is always there. It's a sense of wonder.

About the Author

Adyashanti (whose name means "primordial peace") dares all seekers of peace and freedom to take the possibility of liberation in this life seriously. He began teaching in 1996, at the request of his Zen teacher with whom he had been studying for fourteen years. Since then, many spiritual seekers have awakened to their true nature while spending time with Adyashanti.

The author of *Emptiness Dancing, The Impact of Awakening,* and *My Secret Is Silence,* Adyashanti offers spontaneous and direct nondual teachings that have been compared to those of the early Zen masters and Advaita Vedanta sages. However, Adya says, "If you filter my words through any tradition or '-ism,' you will miss altogether what I am saying. The liberating truth is not static; it is alive. It cannot be put into concepts and be understood by the mind. The truth lies beyond all forms of conceptual fundamentalism. What you are is the beyond—awake and present, here and now already. I am simply helping you to realize that."

A native of Northern California, Adyashanti lives with his wife, Annie, and teaches extensively in the San Francisco Bay Area, offering satsangs, weekend intensives, and silent retreats. He also travels to teach in other areas of the United States and Canada. For more information, please visit www.adyashanti.org.

Additional Sounds True Titles by Adyashanti

Emptiness Dancing
Adyashanti invites readers to wake up to the essence of what we are, through the natural and spontaneous opening of mind, heart, and body that holds the secret to happiness and liberation.

Spontaneous Awakening
Highlights from an extended retreat with Adyashanti, intended to open you to the heart of realization (Audio, 6 CDs).

True Meditation
Adyashanti invites you to reclaim the original purpose of meditation—as a gateway to the objectless freedom of being. Includes three guided meditations (Audio, 3 CDs).

For information about attending events with Adyashanti, as well as a complete selection of books, video recordings, and audio programs by Adyashanti, please visit his Web site: www.adyashanti.org.

About Sounds True

Sounds True was founded in 1985 with a clear vision: to disseminate spiritual wisdom. Located in Boulder, Colorado, Sounds True publishes teaching programs that are designed to educate, uplift, and inspire. With more than six hundred titles available, we work with many of the leading spiritual teachers, thinkers, healers, and visionary artists of our time.

To receive a free catalog of wisdom teachings for the inner life, please visit www.soundstrue.com, call toll-free 800-333-9185, or write: The Sounds True Catalog, P.O. Box 8010, Boulder CO 80306.

SOUNDS TRUE
awakening wisdom